M·A·R·I·L·Y·N

among friends

M·A·R·I·L·Y·N

among friends

SAM SHAW AND NORMAN ROSTEN

CRESCENT BOOKS
New York

This 1992 edition published by CRESCENT BOOKS
distributed by Outlet Book Company Inc., a
Random House Company, 225 Park Avenue South,
New York, New York 10003

Printed in Hong Kong

ISBN 0·517·06989·X

8 7 6 5 4 3 2 1

The photographer Sam Shaw introduced Norman Rosten to Marilyn Monroe in 1955. Their relationship grew: Marilyn's analyst, Dr Ralph Greenson, described Rosten as one of her 'closest friends'. She married another of his friends, Arthur Miller, and from then on saw a great deal of Norman and his wife Hedda. And when she wasn't seeing them, she would phone – at all times of the day and night. Something in the gentle, humorous poet appealed to Marilyn and inspired her trust.

For Rosten, Marilyn was different things at different times: an attractive and vibrant woman, full of fun and energy; an innocent child with an appealing *naiveté*; and, on occasion, a dear friend, badly in need of help.

Photographer Sam Shaw met Monroe on the set of *Viva Zapata* when she was an out-of-work contract player. Shaw was to take many famous photographs of Marilyn, including the skirt-blowing shots for *The Seven-Year Itch*. But he too became her friend and over many years took the kind of photographs that only friends can.

200 of Shaw's intimate photographs, most of them previously unpublished, appear in this book. They reveal many facets of the Marilyn only her true friends knew: the sex goddess ravishing the camera on the beach at Amagansett; the wife shopping with husband Arthur Miller; the woman who longed for children relaxing with Rosten's young daughter Patricia; or the ethereal, virginal nymph dancing innocently among trees.

As her closest friends, both the author and photographer are uniquely placed to reveal the real Marilyn. *Marilyn among Friends* conveys its subject with greater authority, candour and, above all, affection than any previous book.

DEDICATION

To the actress
who strives or dreams
whether at liberty or stardom
taking on her own life and the lives of others
offering magic, pretending miracles

ACKNOWLEDGMENTS

Sam and Marc Weinstein, Color Group Photographic Laboratories

Larry Shaw, Susan Levy, Evelyne Scott-Hansen, Edith Marcus,
Mary Elizabeth Edelman, Mary Leatherbee, Tom Prideaux, Meghan O'Hearn

For permission to reproduce the lines from e.e. cummings' 'Puella Mea'
on p103, Grafton Books, a division of the Collins Publishing Group

CONTENTS

INTRODUCTION

THINGS
TO BE SAID

Marilyn died in 1962; she was thirty-six. Each succeeding generation is drawn to the life and art of this remarkable woman. In half a dozen of her best films, from early walk-ons and one-liners to the emergence of a true comedienne, she left her imprint on cinema history. We keep returning to her life, and the suicide. Grade B melodrama? Greek tragedy? Or American tragedy? Or simply a life not fully realized, the fate of even the noblest strivers?

What more is there to know than the facts already so well known? The illegitimate child, the foster homes, the lure of Hollywood – moth and flame – and the passage of Norma Jean Baker to Marilyn Monroe. Stardom, world fame, marriages and divorce, the body broken, the dissolution of the spirit, and death. Today, we have a resurrection through memory; we have the victory of the pure in heart, the beautiful, and the lost. We take her seriously as an artist and person, a liberated woman before it became fashionable, who won an honored place and lost her life.

We shall leave behind the gossipmongers, journalists and charlatans; the self-proclaimed lovers out of the showbiz swamp; the writers knowingly dispensing fraud; the ex-cooks or ex-maids who sold their secrets (very few); all those who pretended to admire but mocked her decent ambitions; men who would not forgive her turndowns; hungry theorists who found her choice of dying too ordinary or not lucrative enough for the market and speculated on murder, CIA intrigue and Kennedy fantasies; the repeaters of slander and lies from the sexual gutters – her life interpreted, analyzed, pulled apart, pulled together – sensationalizing what were merely human failings. Why the mean-spirited review of her life, long after it was over? She had her share of lovers; she engaged in sex and apparently enjoyed it; she may have slept with one or more of the Kennedys: who's around to confirm or deny? Where and when and ho-hum. We leave that kind of history to the scavengers of the graves of the dead.

Our photographs and words present a woman of obscure beginnings who studied and struggled against great odds to create a life of dignity and respect. She confronted a world of caste and prejudice; she broke into the clear for herself and others.

We who offer this testament liked her, even loved her. We suffered her faults and follies, her tantrums and weaknesses, her difficult days on and off the set, along with her enchanting comic talent. Certain actors and studio executives scorned and vilified her. She had the last hurrah, hers was the joy of being alive and loving her work: the life recalled and held out to us in these sweet, haunting reminders.

1

AT THE
MAKE-UP TABLE

She returns to us as the camera's gift, the treasure of remembrance. She returns in echoes of dark and light, in a truth only the image can yield, the shutter's eye which sees and tells.

The image of Marilyn haunts and flowers from generation to generation. There are not many of her kind. She was born to film, that illusion transforming life into the reality of art.

At the make-up table, out of light and dark, with her brushes and colors, she prepares to enter that other dimension, born of herself. As actress. As magician. As woman. The mystery is hidden in light and shadow, revealed and hidden again, the endless search for identity that is the actor's obsession. Can one become lost in that search, and finally lost to life itself? Was this Marilyn's fate, the inability to hold on to the day-to-day connections with real people and events?

The make-up table. The craft of illusion. The entrance into the labyrinth from which some never return.

The camera loved Marilyn, and she loved the camera, more than her lovers, and husbands, and even her fans.

Half-dressed, she applies her make-up by the light of a tiny lamp with only a 20- or 40-watt bulb. The amber glow forces her to accent eyebrows, lashes, eye shadow, lipstick. The camera and director are waiting outside her dressing room, and farther out in time and space, in movie houses throughout America and the world, her audience waits.

Sam recalls: 'I would say to her, "Marilyn, when I'm shooting you, I don't want to shoot a pretty girl. I want to shoot an actress at work. I want to show how a picture is made – with sweat, struggle, disarrayed hair – to show the evolution of the professional beauty, the professional actress. I want to shoot you at work, at play, as you are. Be free, no phoney poses. Remember the camera loves you and if you wear all that make-up I feel I'm shooting Max Factor, Revlon or Estée Lauder, and not you."'

She says, 'I have a bulbous nose.' And she'd spend three hours before call time on her make-up; her make-up man Whitey Snyder would do the rest. Marilyn was fastidious about certain real or imagined 'defects'. Her nose for one. And her breasts: she did exercises to strengthen them 'to defy gravity', she said.

She had leg worries. She told Sam she had rickets as a child which affected her leg muscles; she was very careful about lighting when she posed. She knew how to control anything bad the camera might reveal; they understood each other very well.

Sam repeats, 'Marilyn, that make-up is a little overdone.'

She replies, 'Sam, you don't understand the public. This make-up is for my fans, those people waiting inside the movie houses, or outside in the street waiting in the crowd at an opening. They are the people the studios won't let close to the theatre unless they pay to get in. When I arrive there I'll turn and wave to them and they'll see me and won't be disappointed. My fans want me to be glamorous. I won't let them down.'

The camera's gift

She'd do things with the shadows on her nose . . .

. . . she knew how to control anything bad the
camera might reveal

AUTHOR CONFERENCE

OK, Sam. She liked to call you Sam Spade. Why the alias?

Her sense of fun. Why did Marilyn call you Claude, for Claude Rains?

Because I was, maybe still am, suave, warm, not bad looking, which was what the real Claude was.

What did she call Eli Wallach, do you know?

Yes, it was Tea House. Eli, you remember, was in *The Tea House of the August Moon* on Broadway. Marilyn loved the title and tagged him with it. I like it. One thing, she referred to me, you and Eli as the three men she most could trust. We were her brothers – she used that word.

So that's how we wind up, eh? As brothers. Okay. Lovers can be a problem. And it's good to have someone's trust.

That's because we were all family men, Sam. Marilyn, who never had a family, or enjoyed family warmth, she got it from us, our wives, and kids.

You think they'd believe us out there?

That's their problem.

Norman, what about her other nicknames?

Well, Arturo was an affectionate tag for Arthur. Poppycock for the dog. She had some cute names for herself, too. She once signed a short note with: 'Noodle, Sam, Max, Clump, Sugar, Finny, Pussy and all the rest.' A game of identity, the playful imp. That was an appealing part of her character. She had a great sense of humor. I think much of her humor comes from early adversity, you know, either it kills you or you can laugh about it. She had a sweet laugh.

This is my favorite

She had this photo in her scrapbook. Written in
multicolored crayon beside it were the words
'This is my favorite'

2

EARLY DAYS

Marilyn was born 'in a trunk' – a backstage baby. Her mother was a wardrobe mistress; years later she said her mother was a film editor. Marilyn wandered in and out of the studios. When she was a kid, it was a closed shop. She was one of them, among friends. The wardrobe departments regarded her as one of their own kind.

When Sam Shaw first met Marilyn, in 1951 or '52, she was unknown. Sam recalls: 'She was a contract player at 20th Century-Fox, on the layoff period until they picked up her contract, two months or so. A darling girl, a darling young woman. She used to drive me to' location when I was covering *Viva Zapata*. Some of the photographs I made of Marilyn when she wasn't known, the post office wouldn't let the magazine they were in (*Argosy*) through the mail. I had given her one

of my sports shirts which she wore open, shirt tails tied at the waist, her cleavage just barely showing. She was wearing a pair of jeans with a frayed fly. I can't get these photographs now: Edward Steichen asked for them and kept them.

'Marilyn once told me she never expected to be a star. She tought she would go from one studio to another, make a rotation of all the studios. She thought she would always be a pretty girl, a starlet. But when Johnny Hyde, her agent and an early lover, discovered her, her world expanded. She studied at UCLA at night, making friends among writers and musicians. At that time, she was like all the young women today, she made her own fashions, ahead of her time. She was among the first to wear jeans. She would get a new pair of jeans from an Army-Navy outlet store,

'She was among the first to wear jeans'

*Wardrobe mistress Ruth and Marilyn –
discussing coffin decor?*

go to Santa Monica beach, go into the sea, drenching the jeans till they clung to her body, then stay in the sun. The jeans dried to her form like a leotard. She said panties would interrupt the flow of the line.

'To me, she wasn't a calendar girl, although Tom Kelly's nude shot was the greatest calendar-type photo. She was a contemporary Aphrodite who could transform herself into a counter girl, a waitress, a beach playmate. She was every teenager we see today in jeans. She could never pour herself into a Cardin, Courrèges or Chanel.'

In those days, when layoff time came up, the studios cut off all monies. As a young starlet, Marilyn couldn't afford changes of clothes to go out on a date or to a dance, but that was never a problem. On call or off salary, the wardrobe department was there to help. Marilyn had the pick of the 20th Century-Fox wardrobe department! True, the gowns were dated and mostly ill-fitting at the bosom. That never bothered her, it amused her. The grips – a very closed sect – also regarded her as one of their own. She often asked them what she could do to add some color to her character;

they would help her improvise a piece of business such as a near-sighted dame who would always bump into furniture when she didn't wear glasses. These men behind the camera had seen every scene-stealing stunt since the silent screen days and knew how to help a buddy of the trade. During make-up time they'd clown and joke; one of their running gags was about the shape she'd use for her coffin and the style of the sheer black négligé she'd be draped in. Whitey was pledged to do the make-up and Ruth (wardrobe) the coffin layout.

Whitey Snyder puts the finishing touches to
Marilyn's make-up

3

THE PRESS,
OR WHY THEY
LOVED HER

In Hollywood, in the late forties, even before she worked for 20th Century-Fox as a starlet, Marilyn and the press got on famously together. She was good copy, and made good cheesecake photos for the girlie mags. She used to drive columnist Sidney Skolsky around to the studios (Sidney didn't drive); he was the first to write stories about her. When she came to New York she met Leonard Lyons who took up where Skolsky left off. They were moving her along, she impressed them. Lyons set up luncheons for her with the then reigning VIPs such as Pulitzer Prize-winning playwright Sidney Kingsley, David Wayne and Richard Adler who recommended her for his musical *The Pajama Game* (she didn't take the part, she felt she wasn't ready). Mary Leatherbee, *Life* movie editor, and Tom Prideaux, *Life* entertainment editor, met her. They were first to print a cover story. *Life* also printed her last interview, by Richard Merriman, taped several days before her death. Marilyn considered it the best ever.

Photographers discovered her – Phillippe Halsman, Richard Avedon, Milton Greene, Bert Stern, Jimmy Kavallines of the *Herald Tribune* – and Marilyn was well on her way. Sam was one of her early discoverers. He introduced her to the *Life* magazine editors and became a faithful friend.

The press followed her antics, delighted in her one-liners, gave her the publicity breaks she needed. Everything seemed to work to her advantage. When the famous nude calendar photo made its appearance in 1949 – an explosive event in that conformist era – the

Studio went into shock. Marilyn defused the issue with her explanation: the human body was nothing to be ashamed of and she had to pay her rent. Who dared to deny the body or the rent? The public loved this stuff.

Cover girl

Her ambition was to appear in Vogue and Harper's Bazaar. *Who else but famous photographer Richard Avedon?*

Look at me

The style at that time was tall, thin and elegant –
Suzy Parker, Dorian Leigh and Anne St Marie.
Marilyn had her own style

She was the darling of columnists such as Walter Winchell and personal friend Earl Wilson, and others. She had the wit and camaraderie to spar with reporters and give them their daily bread: 'Nothing but the radio,' she replied when asked what she had on. She seemed to have the talent and humor to give on-the-spot answers to questions, making it all appear reasonable.

Q: 'What do you wear when you go to bed, Marilyn?'

A: 'Chanel Number Five. Now and then I switch to Arpège.'

Q: 'Do you have any love interest now?'

A: 'No, no serious interests. But I'm always interested.'

Her witticisms were often steeped in a technical knowledge of the business. During the shooting of a scene at a bar in *Bus Stop*, she asked director Josh Logan for a close-up of her. He agreed it was a good moment, but asked, 'How could I shoot a close-up in Cinemascope? [a new method in film photography] I would have to crop off the top of your head.' To which Marilyn replied, 'That's all right. In the previous set-up you established that I have a top to my head.' Even Logan had to join in the laughter.

Set 'em up!

The press made her famous: cynical editors were charmed by this young woman in her late twenties who could hold her own with the pros in the number one drinking-hole in America, the 21 Club

Marilyn giving Broadway columnist Earl Wilson another of her witty one-liners

Bob Kriendler showing Marilyn rare trophies at
the 21 Club

Overleaf:
At Billy Reed's: Marilyn's first outing in New
York City after her 'independence' from
Hollywood, hosted by Leonard Lyons (second
from right). The others, reading from left to
right: David Wayne, Marilyn herself, Milton
Greene, Billy Reed and Sidney Skolsky

Marilyn's first exploration of New York's theatre,
visiting Broadway stars backstage. Here she visits
the late Carole Hainey

Billy Wilder was impressed with her comic talent. He saw her as akin to the Mae West character, and suggested that by creating her unique comedy style she could work in films until she was eighty.

Marilyn had the rare quality of attracting the fascination if not the company of writers and artists: Dylan Thomas, Jackson Pollock, Mark Rothko, Carl Sandburg, Andy Warhol, de Kooning, Tom Wesselman, a host of Monroe watchers. Her era coincided with the emergence of Pop Art: she became their icon, especially in New York.

Director Billy Wilder asked Marilyn to do a 'send-up' of Mae West, satirising Miss West's imitation of gay men. Marilyn, supremely feminine, lacked the element of hostility and ridicule toward men that would be essential in such impersonations. She flunked the test

ON THE TELEPHONE

Sam Spade? Why don't you and Anne meet me for
cocktails at five o'clock in Bungalow Ten at the Beverly
Hills Hotel?

I'm doing a wonderful scene at the Studio with Eli. What
an actor. Have you got a minute? Is Claude around? Keep
an eye on him, he loves you but you know these poets . . .

Hello. Is anybody up? I thought we could meet for coffee
somewhere.
Marilyn, it's 2:30 *AM*
Where's Hedda?
She's asleep. And I will be as soon as I hang up on you,
darlin', much as I hate to do it . . .

Hey, Marlon . . . never mind what am I doin', what are
you doin'? or not doin'? You liked that scene? Lee thought
I was making progress, so maybe I am . . .

C'mon, Josh . . . what've you got against him? He doesn't
look warm enough in that scene? He'll look hot if I can get
closer maybe, I mean, rub-a-dub-dub . . .

No, I can't, I have my head doctor late afternoon, or he
has *my* head, or something. Call me later, alligator!

4

PRIVATE
STAR WARS 1952

Joe DiMaggio did not have a movie smile but a decency showed in his face. That might have attracted Marilyn; she'd had enough of the brash Hollywood type. He was a famous baseball player, a great American athlete, serious, dedicated, well-mannered, light years away from the showbiz sleaze. He may have been over his head with Marilyn, yet he met and pursued – or, as some would have it, was pursued by – and married another 'player' and the world wished them well. They were acclaimed America's Hero and Heroine!

For Marilyn it was a period of preparation for one of her biggest hits, a turning point in her young career, *The Seven Year Itch*. Throughout their relationship, Joe was the star; she became the star after that movie and the divorce that followed. He remained a spectator in a setting where he was never fully at ease. A bittersweet romance at best. But DiMaggio was a gentleman, he never went public with his problems, he never gossiped. One can fairly imagine he suffered in silence.

In 1954, during the Korean War, Marilyn was invited to sing to the American troops. Joe was not very happy about it; he stayed in Tokyo while she went on to Korea. She arrived at the front by helicopter. She recorded it in her own words: 'It was cold and starting to snow. I was backstage in dungarees. Out front the show was on. I could hear music playing and a roar of voices to drown it out. An officer came backstage. "You'll have to go on ahead of schedule. I don't think we can hold them any longer. They're throwing rocks on the stage." The noise I'd been hearing was

my name being yelled by the soldiers. I changed quickly into my silk gown. It had a low neckline and no sleeves. I felt worried all of a sudden about my material, not the Gershwin song but the other I was going to sing – "Diamonds Are A Girl's Best Friend". It seemed like the wrong thing to say to soldiers in Korea, earning only soldier's pay. Then I remembered the dance I would do after the song. It was a cute dance. I knew they would like it.' She confided to columnist Sidney Skolsky upon her return home: 'I felt I belonged . . . I told Joe that for the first time I felt like a movie star.' What Joe had to say about her adventures, we'll never know.

The Seven Year Itch spelt doom for the Marilyn/Joe relationship, for it contained the scene later to be called 'the shot seen round the world' – the famous skirt-blowing episode with Marilyn standing over the sidewalk grating laughingly trying to keep her skirt down and not entirely succeeding, with co-star Tom Ewell looking on bemused and somewhat interested. The draught rising up through the grating was carefully generated by a wind-machine installed below, which also added the subway noise. The area was cordoned off, thousands showed up, well-behaved, enjoying every moment while Marilyn enjoyed it along with the crowd. It was basically a comic scene, but it shocked DiMaggio who was watching the filming that day. He stormed off the set in anger. He was newly married, he didn't like his wife in that situation, yet it was a commonplace Hollywood turn, showing America that their rising star had beautiful legs. Again,

Marilyn and
DiMaggio

On the town in New York, playing the big
leagues

*Johnny Graham (third from left), East Coast
production manager who set up the logistics of
the spectacular scene*

Rehearsing the shot

and not to be forgotten, Marilyn came through as the flower of innocence, sex as good clean fun. America would love it, her, the scene, woman, symbol – the whole package. By next morning it was front page in London, Paris, Rome, Berlin, Tokyo, the whole world. But Joe was clearly unhappy. This was the entertainment capital of the world, fantasyville, peeping-tom land, Hollywood, and you learned to play the game.

Joe's game was baseball.

Marilyn, in her own way, respected his world, and its meaning for him. After their divorce, Joe and Marilyn (on a date) joined Sam and his wife Anne at Manny Wolf's restaurant in New York, on 49th and Third Avenue, a famed steakhouse for sports lovers, basically a man's hangout. On this particular evening, Joe was the special attraction; soon a number of men and their teenage sons stopped by their table, asking for Joe's autograph

on slips of paper, or menu cards. He was the center of attention here. 'The interesting thing,' said Sam about that evening, 'Was Marilyn's attitude. She was proud of Joe, you could tell. She was beaming. She was not in the least bit hurt by watching Joe have his share of glory, you could see she had the highest respect for this man. She didn't know too much about baseball, but she knew he had millions of fans, even as she had. She knew what it must have meant to him, the pride of his art. She could understand that.'

And I could recall a scene in another famous restaurant, Chasen's in Beverly Hills, years after that separation, when my wife and I were joined by Marilyn and her escort William Inge. She had earlier starred in *Bus Stop*, based on Inge's hit play; my accidental meeting with Inge led to this impromptu dinner foursome. Bill Inge, solemn and friendly, was lamenting the decline of the authority of the

screen writer. 'I must have labored on *Bus Stop* for over a year, only to watch it being changed from day to day during the shooting. Then I realized the script is merely a skeleton for the director.' With a courteous ironic smile toward Marilyn, he added, 'And maybe for the actress who loves to add a line or two in her speech.'

Marilyn laughed. 'You writers are always complaining. Why can't we help our character with our own insights, you know, to help what's on the page?'

'Because, dear lady,' Bill replied gently, 'Actors aren't writers, and get paid only to act.'

'I'm hungry, let's order,' said my wife, with her pragmatic wisdom.

'And I don't want to talk shop,' I said, 'Not on this lovely evening in Paradise.'

Marilyn waved to someone across the large room. To our surprise, a man quietly approached our table and greeted her with a slight bow. It was Joe DiMaggio, the second of her three ex-husbands. He gave Inge a curious but not unfriendly stare, putting him instantly at ease. Inge, unhappy at the possibility of being romantically linked with Marilyn, soon relaxed. Joe remained standing as he reached over for Marilyn's hand and pressed it, then turned and acknowledged her introductions. We were all delighted to meet him. One could sense a warm feeling between these two star-crossed lovers. It was a far cry from their dating years, sitting in the Beverly Hills Hotel with Joe's PR buddy, Bernie Kamber, with Joe watching baseball on TV for hours, fol-

Hold the front page!

51st Street, Lexington Avenue, Borough of Manhattan, USA, where the shot seen around the world was taken – front page from New York to California, including London, Paris, Rome, Berlin, Tokyo . . .

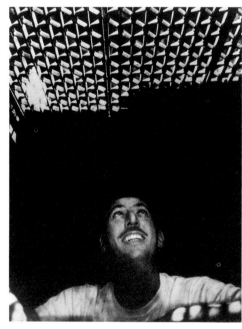

The man who operated the wind-machine under the grating for the skirt-blowing shot

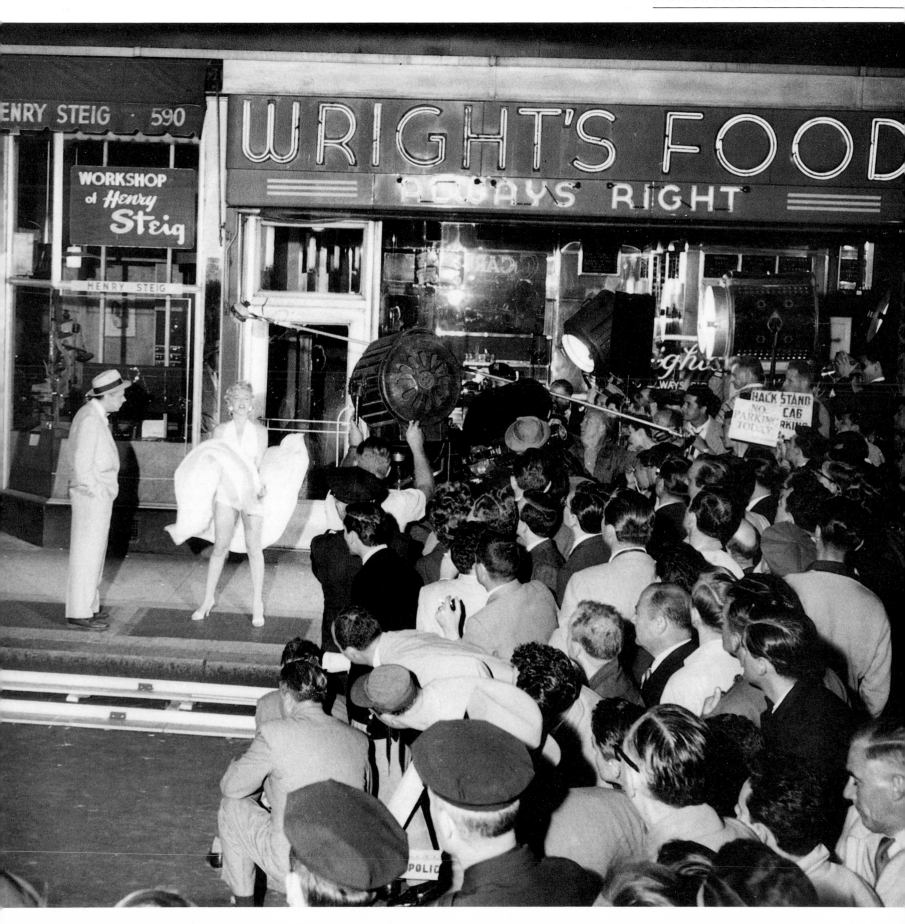

lowed by a stretch of westerns. Marilyn sat next to him all the time, not understanding one play from another, yet desiring his company. It seemed to me, observing them now, that they should have been the happily-ever-after couple among her three marriages. She and Joe had a similar street-smart air, a tough instinct for survival, that might have served them well in the years to come. But a longing in her stirred to the music of a different drummer, a music that led her to a more ambitious and dangerous love. Miller, like DiMaggio, was a quiet man, with deep inner drives, centered less on others than on himself. And Marilyn, looking for a safe haven, turned toward him and the perilous adventures of art.

But at that moment, with Joe standing by, asking her about her new film in preparation, he appeared a steadfast friend. His fist playfully against her jaw, he said, 'Best of luck, kid. You have what it takes.' Yet he knew, this athlete who set a record of consecutive base hits in a glorious career, that every string must run out.

5

'ACTOR'S TRUTH'

On a film set, a 'nude' actor, say under a bedsheet, generally wore underwear. Such precautions were taken in case the covering should accidentally be whisked off by a prop person. Horrors! Nudity in a town where nudity is unknown!

Or, in a bathtub, the actress (men are rarely seen in baths, usually in macho showers) might be required suddenly to change position or rise abruptly. Horrors again in a town where a soap-covered female nude is a sacrilege! Thus, even in a bubble-bath shot, a few emergency clothing items were worn.

But Marilyn insisted on being nude under the coverings. She wanted 'to be true to the situation and character.' She called it 'actor's truth'. This attitude was instinctive and not as a result of the Method or her tuition from the master teachers Michael Chekhov and Lee Strasberg. She was great on instinct. She asked, 'Would *you* take a bath, bubble or not, wearing panties and a bra?'

Nude in real life, nude beneath the suds! While Victor Moore, who played a plumber in *The Seven Year Itch*, looked on and seemed to enjoy it.

Don't peek!

Marilyn between takes (with cinematographer Milton Krasner in the background)

Acting coach Natasha Lytess takes Marilyn
through her lines

That's not fair!

Billy Wilder sneaks a kiss from a captive Marilyn

6

THE GIRL WITH
NO NAME

Film writer George Axelrod said: 'I have seen at least twenty different actresses play the part of the Girl in my play *The Seven Year Itch*. I have seen the Girl as a blonde, a brunette, and a redhead. I've heard her say her lines with a British accent, in French, in Italian, in German. Many of the actresses have been wonderful in the part. A few have been a little less wonderful. But only one has ever come really close to playing the part exactly the way I imagined it when I first wrote it.

'Marilyn Monroe doesn't just play the Girl. She *is* the Girl. Marilyn once told me that playing the part had helped her to find out who she was. Which is a pretty nice thing for a writer to hear from an actress.

'I am revealing no breathtaking secret when I say that Marilyn has a reputation for not being the easiest actress in the world to work with. Her eagerness and ambition cause her to tense up. She has difficulty remembering lines. She has been known to drive directors stark, raving mad. However, an interesting thing happened during the shooting of *Itch*. My favorite scene in the picture comes close to the end. It is a kind of serious and extremely difficult scene in which the Girl explains to the hero (who, to all outward appearances, is the least dashing, least glamorous, least romantic man alive) why she finds him exciting and attractive and why his wife has every reason to be jealous.

'Because of its difficulty and the fact that it ends with a long speech from the Girl, it was generally assumed that the scene would need several days to get on film. Billy Wilder

Scenes on the set of The Seven Year Itch

patiently struggled through dozens of takes for every scene except this one. Three minutes later it was all over. Marilyn had done it, letter perfect and with an emotional impact that caused the entire soundstage to burst into applause at the end, on the first take. There was no need for a second.

'She told me later she was able to do the scene because she believed every word of what she was saying and because it seemed to her like the story of her own life. As it might be interesting to see what it is that Marilyn so firmly believed in, here's the end of the scene as it appears in the shooting script:

(SCENE 85. LIVINGROOM. DAY. TWO SHOT. RICHARD AND THE GIRL)

RICHARD

Let's face it – no pretty girl in her right mind wants *me*. She wants Gregory Peck...

THE GIRL

How do you know what a pretty girl wants? You think every pretty girl is a dope. You think that a girl goes to a party and there is some guy – a great big hunk in a fancy striped vest, strutting around like a tiger – giving you that 'I'm so handsome, you can't resist me' look – and from this she is supposed to fall flat on her face. Well, she doesn't fall flat on her face. But there's another guy in the room... way over in the corner... maybe he's kind of nervous and shy and perspiring a little... First you look past him, but then you sort of sense that he is gentle and kind and worried, that he'll be tender with you and nice and

sweet, and that's what's really exciting!

If I were your wife, I'd be jealous of you... I'd be very, very jealous.

(She kisses him)

I think you're just elegant!

'I have been asked if there is any symbolic significance in the fact that the Girl has no name. The truth of the matter is that I could never think of a name for her that seemed exactly right, that really fit the girl I had in mind. I think if I were writing the play today, I might be tempted to call the Girl Marilyn.'

Commercial break

In the midst of meeting production schedules of
$10,000 a day, Billy Wilder stops for a reflective
moment before filming a satire on TV
commercials which holds up very well today

Phew!
Marilyn cooling off

Marilyn posing with a young man for a publicity still

Tiger Lily

. . . la femme fatale

Candid moments on the set

Old Fashioned Hollywood

Booms, lights, cameras, grips and gaffers up in the grids, to capture a single moment in the life of a film

When she met Clark Gable, Marilyn was as thrilled as any teenager. They were seated together at the same table, the King and the new princess. Her biggest thrill was asking for and getting Gable's autograph, 'the autograph I wanted since I was twelve years old,' she told him. Her costume was from 20th Century wardrobe – she didn't own a formal gown – and she had borrowed jewelry from Mrs Karger, the 'grande dame' of Hollywood society, so real they looked like real fakes.

Sam recalls: 'Tommy Ewell's and my hired tuxedos and patent leather shoes were from Western Costume: sewn pockets, no money, shoes too big. The maturing/aging beauties of Hollywood and the producers' wives wouldn't allow bright lights, only romantic candlelight glow. I had to borrow a flash camera from *Life* photographer Jack Birns. On the way to the party, neither Marilyn nor I had any money. Marilyn was high. It was the night of her life. No gas in the tank, she sweet-talked a gas station attendant for gas. In the doorway of the restaurant, a crowd of fans waited for her. She kept all the star-studded guests waiting inside while she posed for her fans who photographed her with their amateur cameras.'

Here's to you, my dear

Producer Charles Feldman toasting the new star
with Jean Howard and Clark Gable
eavesdropping

*The autograph she wanted 'since I was twelve
years old'*

Agent Ned Marin with Susan Hayward and
Clifton Webb

French ballet stars Zizi Jean Maire and Roland Petit

Michael Rennie and Lauren Bacall

George Burns and a Swedish starlet, unidentified

Gary Cooper and Hjordis Tersmeden

Marilyn danced with the handsome and powerful: with Clark Gable and Humphrey Bogart, Darryl Zanuck and Clifton Webb; she danced with new friends and old. 'As I watched and photographed in the low-key light of Romanoff's, it struck me that she was a metaphor of Hollywood, a place of corny pictures, monstrous business people, monster movies, but also of serious film-makers, producers, writers, directors, actors, camera and crew men – all of them wanting to do their best. Marilyn kept wanting and trying to do her best.' This was an evening of triumph and high hopes for the future. As Marilyn would say later on, 'After all, I have come from way down.'

This was one of her 'up' moments.

Definitely.

Star and producer

Cutting up with Clifton Webb

Clark and Marilyn: Dancing in the Dark

Lauren Bacall and agent extraordinaire Irving Swifty Lazar

Sam and Marilyn backstage

12

POPCORN
AND HUZZAH

Marilyn liked people and crowds – she was definitely not the recluse type – but some who accompanied her on public missions did not. I did not. She confided that crowds could be scary, yet she knew their power in her behalf: '. . . and I want to say that the people – if I am a star – the people made me a star. No studio, no person, but the people did.'

It is well to keep in mind that she came out of neighborhoods of working people (she worked in a factory during World War II), the kind she could trust, the kind who would later come to her movies just to see her smile, and walk, and turn with a flick of her hips that was naughty but nice. Few, if any, movie stars gained such mass reactions, not Ava Gardner, Elizabeth Taylor or even the great Garbo. Hers was the popcorn and huzzah crowd. Later though, with fame, she proved she could mingle easily with all levels of society, from the Queen of England (during the filming of *The Prince and the Showgirl* in London), personalities as varied as Dame Edith Sitwell and Isak Dinesen (Karen Blixen), and the American poet Carl Sandburg, to the doorman of her building, and the crowds, the anonymous ticket-buyers, all those from whom she derived her energy and confidence. She took to publicity with ease, whether welcoming the Israeli soccer team to glorious Ebbets Field in Brooklyn or being welcomed by airport mechanics in their work clothes.

Hi there!

She greets the crowds whom she loves so much

Her body is most beauteous
being for all things amorous
fashioned very curiously
of roses and of ivory

e.e.cummings

13

LOVE IN THE CITY

It began, as most love stories begin, in the entranced light of youthful happiness. Arthur Miller and Marilyn Monroe fell in love. They were young, already famous, with Marilyn ready for the most dramatic step of her career. She had just gone through a painful separation from DiMaggio; now salvation beckoned with Miller.

How to explain this awesome, improbable event? Body meeting Mind? Beauty and the Beast? Cleopatra and Antony? Power attracting power? All sorts of theories emerged. Those who tried, both then and now, to explain it soon realized how futile was their task. Let the experts, Freudians, Jungians, mystics, astrologists, or psychiatrists as well explain smoke. Or music. The dumb-blonde image was dead and gone, for certain.

The outdoor wedding took place on July 1st, 1956 in a rural Connecticut village. It was an orthodox Jewish ceremony with the bride recently converted to Judaism, her own mysterious wish. A lawn party on a glorious summer day, with perhaps twenty-five guests and relatives, very few reporters, and all giddy with anticipation and beverage. The bride was beautiful, the groom handsome and looking quite orderly for a writer. They did all the proper things, they laughed, kissed one another repeatedly and allowed themselves to be kissed, drank champagne (the bride's favorite intake), and answered the ridiculous questions always asked at weddings.

I was supposed to be the best man but was bumped at the last moment by a late-arriving relative. (Marilyn gave me an additional kiss for this snub and whispered, 'Don't worry about it.') Mild chaos hovered over the event, not enough to spoil the sweet sense of happiness-to-come. The ceremony began. Observing the Jewish ritual, Marilyn lifted her veil to sip from a goblet of wine, at the same time (I may be recalling this in the wrong order) breaking the ceremonial glass with her foot. She said 'I do' like in the movies, they exchanged rings; the rest is foggy except the day was glorious and more like music than merely weather. The only sad note was revealed to us later: two reporters from *Paris Match*, speeding to the wedding on a motorcycle, crashed some miles off and one was killed.

At the beginning, then, a tender romance with New York City as their playground. The newlyweds both loved the city, the early months of their marriage were celebrated in their Sutton Place apartment and the adjoining terrain: Central Park, further downtown, even a Brooklyn home visit! They were walkers, and surprised themselves by being good conversationalists; it was an idyllic interlude in what would slowly become the stressful adjustment of two people dancing around the showbiz volcano. Given the life and ambitions of the principals, it was hard not to predict trouble. Careers clashing with personal needs: the writer's desire for privacy and silence, the actor needing an audience and adulation.

At this point in his career (1955-56), Miller was under a political cloud. The clown act periodically playing Washington D.C. to alert the populace to the threat of subversion decided he was important enough to attract

Go faster!

Lovers in the left lane

'Never the twain . . .'

. . . but they did

the media, especially with Marilyn in the picture. Communist hunters Senator Joseph McCarthy and Representative Francis Walter sniffed the air. Miller was called to testify before the House committee, joined by Marilyn who appeared with him publicly in defiance of the bad guys (she turned everything into a movie). He denied any connection with 'communist' groups, which prompted Rep. Walter to utter some priceless prose: 'I don't see how we can consistently not cite him because he very obviously is in contempt.' Whereupon Miller, the dramatist, outflanked him. In reply to Walter's question, 'What is your objective in going to England?' (Miller had applied earlier for a passport to accompany Marilyn for her projected film with Olivier), Miller tossed his grenade. 'My objective is double,' he replied, 'I wish to attend a production of my play, and to be with the woman who will then be my wife.'

What a curtain line! Even Marilyn was taken by surprise. Walter staggered off to the cloakroom. To lose to a mere writer! For the image of a dangerous activist had suddenly turned into that of a lover, and lovers are of course incapable of political action (Byron excepted). And who ever heard of a romantic communist? It was clearly an error. Congressman Walter, then up for re-election, added a touch of farce to the comedy. He requested to be photographed with Miss Monroe. Request denied.

The play referred to by Miller was *A View From The Bridge*, first produced in New York and later in London. It became a big success

Marilyn rowing at New York's most romantic
rendezvous, Central Park lake

The Hollywood ending, foretold

there, and it had a long run.

Soon after the wedding ceremony, which took place in the summer of '56 in a barrage of publicity, Marilyn flew off to England for part-honeymoon and part-work (it turned out to be mostly all work) as she starred with Laurence Olivier in the filming of *The Prince and the Showgirl*. The picture was a success, and vaulted Marilyn to a new level of stardom, linked with the most illustrious classical actor of the time. It was not a happy relationship – the Actor's Studio method was not exactly Olivier's – but it proved that Marilyn, newly launched from the East (non-Hollywood) coast, was developing as a self-confident comedienne, a role she handled with high skill in her later and next to last film, *Some Like It Hot*.

Back to Hollywood and domestic living in the celluloid jungle, with Miller trying to concentrate on his writing; the East-West shuttle, the pressure of careers, hers and his, continuing . . .

Love eternal was to last a mere five years.

Dark nightmares and romantic obsession

AUTHOR CONFERENCE

Certain commentators, women especially, say that Marilyn was a 'victim' of the Hollywood system. How do you feel about that, Sam?

I don't agree.

Neither do I, it's too easy.

You can say that she was crushed by forces beyond her control, personal weaknesses, drugs and pills. That isn't the same as being a victim. At the beginning, maybe you could use that word, low pay, all kinds of hours, industry exploitation . . .

I think women want to use her as a symbol, to evoke sympathy through her struggle and, rightly so, given the cultural and economic factors, to see it as a political thing.

But you know, Norman – we've both lived through it – that Marilyn fought back, something your ordinary victim doesn't do. She fought the studio and its contract tyranny, she fought for and won small but important victories, such as script approval, choice of director, other controls . . . you can't call her a victim, period. It isn't simple with Marilyn. Nothing is.

17

MARILYN LOVES HUGO AND VICE VERSA

It may have seemed like Beauty and the Beast to some, but Marilyn and Hugo loved one another deeply. She worried about her basset hound, especially about his depressions. Her doctor told her that animals can sometimes be cheered up by a small shot of whiskey.

Did Handsome Hugo like the hard stuff? He never said, but he's been seen (I have seen him) on more than one occasion to swallow a teaspoon of eighty-six proof tenderly administered by Marilyn. He would then stand still, turn, stare, sneeze, and do a kind of wobbly dance, possibly even offer a smile, which bassets rarely do. Whatever it was, he swallowed, and the days of his dogdom were lightened.

Marilyn's worries may have been induced by Hugo's peculiar doggie hazards, such as, for instance, how to put it . . . the basset, as you may know, is a low-slung animal, moving close to the ground. Marilyn was anxious (she confided to me) that in hurrying over the rocky country terrain of their farm, Hugo's low penis might possibly strike a stone. She'd cry out merrily, 'Be careful, Hugo!'

She had once written a fragment entitled 'To The Weeping Willow', with these lines:

I stood beneath your limbs
and you flowered and finally clung to me
and when the wind struck with . . . the earth
and sand – you clung to me

She often tried her hand at poetry. It was her way of saying difficult things to herself. If we read limbs as 'branches', she had her wish in death: she became one with nature.

192 EPILOGUE: A BACKWARD LOOK

EPILOGUE: A BACKWARD LOOK

Marilyn often referred to me as her 'closest friend'. I'm not sure what 'closest' means. I was not her lover. I thought of myself and my wife Hedda as a single supportive force toward a sweet but troubled human being. My wife believed I loved Marilyn; but so did she. If love is that force, or presence, we both did. We were at peace with that idea. Possibly it was the love of a parent for a child, an older daughter, or a family member whose life was on the wrong track.

In those years, people, friends, were closer. There was more meaning to friend-ship. Today, the pursuit of happiness is more brutally the pursuit of power, its seekers trusting in things rather than feelings. People like Marilyn never quite made it from power to happiness. She had the instinct and reflexes of the poet, but lacked the control.

She was a beautiful, almost other-worldly creature who left behind some of that beauty. And I, the last of that trio, thank her for a brief visitation into our lives.